The Ultimate SMOOTHIE RECIPE BOOK

By
Les Ilagan

Les Ilagan

*Copyright © CONTENT ARCADE PUBLISHING. All rights reserved.
This recipe book is copyright protected and meant for personal use only.
No part of this recipe book may be used, paraphrased, reproduced, scanned, distributed or sold in any printed or electronic form without permission of the author and the publishing company.
Copying pages or any part of this recipe book for any purpose other than own personal use is prohibited and would also mean violation of copyright law.*

DISCLAIMER

Content Arcade Publishing and its authors are joined together in their efforts in creating these pages and their publications. Content Arcade Publishing and its authors make no assurance of any kind, stated or implied, with respect to the information provided.

LIMITS OF LIABILITY

Content Arcade Publishing and its authors shall not be held legally responsible in the event of incidental or consequential damages in line with, or arising out of, the supplying of the information presented here.

Table of Contents

Introduction 7

So now, let's get started! 8

Mango Orange and Strawberry Smoothie . 9

AvocadoAlmond and Yogurt Smoothie 11

Blackberry Strawberry and Coconut Smoothie 13

Blueberry Banana and Ricotta Smoothie 15

Spiced Raspberry Yogurt and Soy Smoothie 17

Almond Cherry and Banana Smoothie with Hemp Seeds 19

Banana Cottage Cheese and Vanilla Smoothie 21

Banana Blueberries and Soy Smoothie with Flaxseed 23

Grape Kiwi and Cranberry Smoothie 25

Banana Kiwi and Green Tea Smoothie 27

Lychee Melon and Vanilla Smoothie 29

Banana Peach and Oat Smoothie 31

Creamy Mango-Apricot Smoothie with Cinnamon 33

Mango Ginger and Wheatgrass Smoothie 35

Mango and Orange Smoothie with Hemp Seed 37

Mixed Berry Banana and Soy Smoothie ... 39

Berry Kiwi and Lemon Smoothie 41

Papaya Orange and Carrot Smoothie 43

Papaya Banana and Pine Cooler 45

Raspberry Watermelon and Yogurt Smoothie 47

Fig Banana and Cashew Smoothie 49

Red Currant Cranberry and Yogurt Delight 51

Minty Strawberry and Yogurt Smoothie .. 53

Pear Raspberry and Ricotta Smoothie 55

Yummy Strawberry Ricotta Cooler 57

Apple Banana and Peanut Butter Smoothie 59

Banana Strawberry and Flax Smoothie ... 61

Easy Mango Cheesecake Smoothie 63

Banana Strawberry Cereal and Yogurt Smoothie 65

Blackberry Almond and Oat Cooler 67

Delightful Tofu Banana and Cinnamon Smoothie 69

Strawberry Kiwi Milkshake 71

Berry Apple and Orange Smoothie 73

Delicious and Healthy Green Smoothie ...75

Black Currant Banana and Almond Smoothie 77

Easy Cardamom Raspberry and Pear Smoothie 79

Banana Cucumber Radish Smoothie with Parsley 81

Peach Banana and Cottage Cheese Smoothie 83

Kiwi Banana Smoothie with Pumpkin Seed 85

Raspberry Cucumber and Rhubarb Smoothie 87

Purple Berry Smoothie 89

Quick and Easy Fruit Cooler 91

Fruit Cereal and Almond Smoothie 93

Luscious Banana-Mango Yogurt Smoothie 95

Almond Mango and Dragon Fruit Smoothie 97

Pineapple Mango and Coconut Smoothie 99

Pineapple Peach and Coconut Smoothie 101

Beet Dragon Fruit and Coconut Smoothie with Chia 103

Vegan Strawberry Smoothie with Walnuts 105

Cranberry Soy Breakfast Smoothie 107

Dark Choco Banana and Peanut Butter Smoothie 109

Watermelon Coconut Smoothie with Hemp Seed 111

Papaya Citrus Cooler with Honey 113

Peach Strawberry and Almond Smoothie with Flax 115

Breakfast Choco Banana Protein Smoothie 117

Easy Avocado Soy and Maple Smoothie .119

Strawberry Plum and Coconut Smoothie with Chia 121

Introduction

This book has a wide selection of smoothie recipes that you can enjoy anytime of the day.

Smoothies are very easy to make. You only need a liquid base(milk, yogurt, fruit juice, or water), some fruits or vegetables, a bit of seeds or nuts if desired, and of course a good blender.

Smoothies are very versatile. You can mix and match some of the ingredients or add more depending on your taste and health requirement. For some people that can't take dairies, there are other options that are equally delicious and nutritious like soy-based milk or yogurt, rice milk, almond milk, and coconut milk.

They are also fun to make because you can add any ingredient that you desire. Even your kids can help you in making them because the process is very easy and simple, you just need to put everything in your blender and there you have it – a refreshing drink in less than 5 minutes!

Smoothies are for everyone to enjoy. By drinking a glass or two a day can ensure that you are getting enough vitamins and minerals that your body needs. It is also a good way of using your fruits and vegetables since they are highly perishable. Strawberries, bananas, and milk are common smoothie ingredients that are easily found in supermarkets. Feel free to browse on the recipes on this book and for sure you can whip something good out of these simple yet delicious ingredients.

Read on and I hope you enjoy all the recipes in this book.

So now, let's get started!

Mango Orange and Strawberry Smoothie

This scrumptious smoothie recipe with apple, orange, and strawberry has just the right amount of sweet-tangy flavors.

Preparation Time: 5 minutes
Total Time: 5 minutes
Yield: 2 servings

Ingredients
1 medium mango
1 medium seedless orange

8medium strawberries
1 cup of milk
1 cup ice cubes

Method

1.   Peel both the mango and the orange and cut them into small pieces.
2.   Hull the strawberries and also cut them into small pieces.
3.   Put them in the blender along with the milk and ice cubes.
4.   Blend until smooth and pour into serving glasses.
5.   Serve immediately and enjoy.

AvocadoAlmond and Yogurt Smoothie

This is a power packed smoothie recipe that combines the flavor of avocado, almond, yogurt, and honey.

Preparation Time: 5 minutes
Total Time: 5 minutes
Yield: 3 servings

Ingredients
1 medium avocado
1 1/2 cup of almond milk

1 cup of plain or vanilla-flavored yogurt
1 Tbsp. honey
1 cup ice cubes

Method

1.	Remove and discard pit from avocado. Cut into small pieces and place into the blender along with the almond milk, yogurt, honey, and ice cubes.
2.	Blend until smooth then transfer into 3 chilled tall glasses.
3.	Serve immediately and enjoy.

Blackberry Strawberry and Coconut Smoothie

This smoothie recipe with blackberries, strawberries, milk, coconut, and honey is so delicious!

Preparation Time: 5 minutes
Total Time: 5 minutes
Yield: 2 servings

Ingredients
1/2 cup frozen blackberries
1/2 cup frozen strawberries
1/2 cup skim milk
1/2 cup coconut water
2 Tbsp. Coconut butter
1 Tbsp. honey

Method
1. Place the blackberries, strawberries, skim milk, coconut water, and coconut butter in a blender. Process until smooth and combined well.
2. Divide smoothie among 2 chilled glasses.
3. Serve with a straw and garnish with berries, if desired.

Blueberry Banana and Ricotta Smoothie

This quick and easy smoothie recipe is made with blueberries, banana, ricotta, and skim milk.

Preparation Time: 5 minutes
Total Time: 5 minutes
Yield: 2 servings

Ingredients
1 medium frozen banana (cut into small pieces)
1 cup frozen blueberries
1 cup skim milk
1/2 cup ricotta cheese
fresh mint sprigs

Method
1. Combine the banana, blueberries, skim milk, and ricotta cheese in a blender. Process until it becomes smooth.
2. Pour mixture into two chilled glasses. Garnish with fresh mint sprigs.
3. Serve and enjoy.

Spiced Raspberry Yogurt and Soy Smoothie

This mildly spiced pink smoothie recipe is so tasty and healthy too!

Preparation Time: 5 minutes
Total Time: 5 minutes
Yield: 2 servings

Ingredients
1 cup of frozen raspberries
6 oz. Greek yogurt
1 cup soy milk
1/4 teaspoon cinnamon
1/4 teaspoon ground nutmeg
fresh mint sprig

Method
1.	Place the raspberries, yogurt, soy milk, cinnamon, and nutmeg in a blender. Process until smooth and creamy.
2.	Divide smoothie in 2 chilled glasses. Garnish with some raspberries and mint sprig, if desired.
3.	Serve and enjoy.

Almond Cherry and Banana Smoothie with Hemp Seeds

This is a wonderful smoothie recipe that combines the flavor of almond, cherry, banana, and hemp seeds.

Preparation Time: 5 minutes
Total Time: 5 minutes
Yield: 2 servings

Ingredients
1 cup frozen cherries (pitted)
1 medium frozen banana (cut into small pieces)
1 ½ cup almond milk
2 tsp. hemp seeds
fresh mint sprigs

Method
1. Combine the cherries, banana, almond milk, and hemp seeds in a blender. Process until it becomes smooth.
2. Pour smoothie in 2 chilled glasses. Garnish with some cherries and mint sprigs, if desired.
3. Serve and enjoy.

Banana Cottage Cheese and Vanilla Smoothie

This rich and creamy smoothie recipe with banana and cottage cheese is perfect for breakfast or snack.

Preparation Time: 5 minutes
Total Time: 5 minutes
Yield: 2 servings

Ingredients

2 medium frozen banana, cut into small pieces
1/2 cup cottage cheese
11/2 cup skim milk
2 tsp. honey

Method

1. Place the banana, cottage cheese, skim milk, and honey ice in a blender. Process until smooth and creamy.
2. Pour and divide among 2 chilled glasses.
3. Serve immediately and enjoy.

Banana Blueberries and Soy Smoothie with Flaxseed

This delightful smoothie made with banana, blueberries, soy milk, and flax is so rich in flavor and nutrients.

Preparation Time: 5 minutes
Total Time: 5 minutes
Yield: 2 servings

Ingredients
1 medium frozen banana (cut into small pieces)
1 cup frozen blueberries
1 cup soy milk
1/2 cup soy yogurt
1 Tbsp. flaxseeds
fresh mint sprigs

Method
1. Place the banana, blueberries, soy milk, soy yogurt, and flaxseeds in a blender. Process until smooth and creamy.
2. Pour smoothie in 2 chilled glasses. Garnish with some blueberries and fresh mint sprig, if desired.
3. Serve and enjoy.

Grape Kiwi and Cranberry Smoothie

This refreshing smoothie with grapes, kiwi, and cranberry is very easy to prepare.

Preparation Time: 5 minutes
Total Time: 5 minutes
Yield: 2 servings

Ingredients
1 cup of seedless grapes
2 medium kiwi fruit (peeled and cut into small pieces)
1 cup cranberry juice
1 cup of ice cubes
fresh mint sprig

Method
1. Place the grapes, kiwi, cranberry juice, and ice cubes in a blender. Process until smooth.
2. Pour and divide among 2 chilled glasses. Garnish with mint sprig, if desired.
3. Serve and enjoy.

Banana Kiwi and Green Tea Smoothie

This flavorful green smoothie recipe with banana, kiwi, kale, and green tea will give you loads of antioxidants and fiber to keep you healthy and strong.

Preparation Time: 5 minutes
Total Time: 5 minutes
Yield: 2 servings

Ingredients
2 medium frozen bananas (cut into small pieces)
2 medium kiwi fruit (peeled and cubed)
1 cup of kale (torn)
1 cup of freshly brewed green tea
1/2 cup of crushed ice

Method
1.   Combine the banana, kiwi, kale, green tea, and crushed ice in a blender.
2.   Blend everything together until smooth.
3.   Pour into two glasses and serve immediately.

Lychee Melon and Vanilla Smoothie

This smoothie recipe with lychees, melon, and vanilla is so refreshing!

Preparation Time: 5 minutes
Total Time: 5 minutes
Yield: 3 servings

Ingredients
1 cup lychees (peeled and pitted)
1 cuprock melon (peeled, deseeded, and diced)
1 cup skim milk
1 cup ice cubes
1/4 tsp. vanilla extract
fresh mint sprigs

Method
1.	Combine the lychees, rock melon, skim milk, ice cubes, and vanilla extract in a blender. Process until it becomes smooth.
2.	Pour and divide smoothie among 3 chilled glasses. Garnish fresh mint sprigs.
3.	Serve immediately and enjoy.

Banana Peach and Oat Smoothie

This wonderful smoothie is packed with good for you nutrients from the banana, peach and rolled oats.

Preparation Time: 5 minutes
Total Time: 5 minutes
Yield: 2 servings

Ingredients
1 medium frozen banana (cut into small pieces)
2 cups skim milk
2 peach halves
2 Tbsp. rolled oats
fresh mint sprigs

Method
1.	Place the banana, skim milk, peach halves, and oats in a blender. Process until smooth and creamy.
2.	Pour in 2 chilled glasses. Garnish with banana slices, some oats, and mint sprigs, if desired.
3.	Serve immediately and enjoy.

Creamy Mango-Apricot Smoothie with Cinnamon

Mango and apricot are naturally sweet which makes this smoothie taste heavenly.

Preparation Time: 5 minutes
Total Time: 5 minutes
Yield: 3 servings

Ingredients

1 cup mango (cut into cubes)
4 apricots (pitted and halved)
1 cup skim milk
1/2 cup vanilla yogurt
1/4 tsp. cinnamon (ground)
1 cup crushed ice

Method

1. Combine the mango, apricots, skim milk, yogurt, cinnamon, and crushed ice in a blender. Process until it becomes smooth.
2. Pour and divide smoothie among 3 chilled glasses. Garnish with a small slice of mango and sprinkle with more cinnamon, if desired.
3. Serve immediately and enjoy.

Mango Ginger and Wheatgrass Smoothie

A yummy treat when you are not feeling well. This smoothie is loaded with nutrients that can help you recover fast from sickness.

Preparation Time: 5 minutes
Total Time: 5 minutes
Yield: 2 servings

Ingredients
1 cup frozen mango
2 tsp. wheatgrass powder
2 Tbsp. lemon juice
1/4 tsp. ground ginger
1 cup coconut water
1 cup ice cubes

Method
1. Combine the mango, wheat grass powder, lemon juice, ginger, and coconut water in a blender. Process for 20 seconds or until blended well.
2. Add the ice cubes and blend again until it becomes smooth.
3. Pour and divide smoothie among 2 chilled glasses.
4. Serve and enjoy.

Mango and Orange Smoothie with Hemp Seed

This smoothie recipe with mango, orange, and hemp seeds is not only refreshing but also loaded with nutrients.

Preparation Time: 5 minutes
Total Time: 5 minutes
Yield: 2 servings

Ingredients
1 cup mango (diced)
1/2 cup of orange juice
1/2 cup Greek yogurt
2 tsp. hemp seeds
1 cup ice cubes
fresh mint sprigs

Method
1. Combine mango, orange juice, yogurt, hemp seeds, and ice cubes in your blender. Process until smooth.
2. Pour and divide smoothie among 2 chilled glasses.
3. Serve and enjoy.

Mixed Berry Banana and Soy Smoothie

This delightful smoothie recipe with mixed berries, banana, and soy milk makes a fantastic afternoon pick-me-up!

Preparation Time: 5 minutes
Total Time: 5 minutes
Yield: 2 servings

Ingredients
1 cup frozen mixed berries
1 medium frozen banana (cut into small pieces)
11/2 cup soy milk
fresh mint sprigs

Method
1.	Place the mixed berries, banana, and soy milk in a high-speed blender. Process until smooth and creamy.
2.	Pour in 2 chilled glasses. Garnish with a few blueberries and mint sprigs, if desired.
3.	Serve and enjoy!

Berry Kiwi and Lemon Smoothie

Healthy and delicious. You can never go wrong with this combination.

Preparation Time: 5 minutes
Total Time: 5 minutes
Yield: 2 servings

Ingredients
1cup frozen mixed berries
1 medium kiwi fruit(diced)

1 cup skim milk
2 Tbsp. lemon juice
1 Tbsp. honey
1/2 cup crushed ice
lemon wedges
fresh mint sprigs

Method

1.   Place the mixed berries, kiwi fruit, skim milk, lemon juice, honey, and ice in a blender. Process until it becomes smooth.
2.   Pour and divide smoothie among 2 serving glasses. Garnish with lemon wedges and fresh mint sprig, if desired
3.   Serve immediately and enjoy.

Papaya Orange and Carrot Smoothie

Looking for a healthy smoothie that also taste yummy? Try this recipe!

Preparation Time: 5 minutes
Total Time: 5 minutes
Yield: 2 servings

Ingredients
1 cup of papaya (cubed)
1 medium seedless orange (peeled and cut into segments)
3/4 cup carrot juice
1 cup of ice cubes

Method
1. Place the papaya, orange, carrot juice, and ice cubes in a high-speed blender. Process until it becomes smooth.
2. Pour mixture in 2 chilled glasses. Garnish with a slice of orange, if desired.
3. Serve immediately and enjoy.

Papaya Banana and Pine Cooler

A refreshing blend of tropical flavors in one amazing drink!

Preparation Time: 5 minutes
Total Time: 5 minutes
Yield: 2 servings

Ingredients

1 cup papaya (cubed)
1 medium frozen banana (cut into small pieces)
1/2 cup pineapple tidbits
1/2 cup skim milk
2 Tbsp. coconut cream
1 cup crushed ice
fresh mint sprigs

Method

1.	Place the papaya, banana, pineapple tidbits, skim milk, coconut cream, and crushed ice in a blender. Process until it becomes smooth.
2.	Pour in 2 chilled glasses. Garnish with fresh mint sprigs.
3.	Serve and enjoy!

Raspberry Watermelon and Yogurt Smoothie

This smoothie recipe with raspberries, watermelon, and yogurt is very satisfying.

Preparation Time: 5 minutes
Total Time: 5 minutes
Yield: 2 servings

Ingredients
1 cup frozen raspberries
1 cup watermelon

6 oz. Greek yogurt
1/2 cup low-fat milk
fresh mint sprigs

Method

1. Place the raspberries, watermelon, yogurt, and milk in a blender. Process until smooth.
2. Pour in 2 chilled glasses. Garnish with fresh mint sprigs.
3. Serve and enjoy. Recipe may be doubled if serving many people.

Fig Banana and Cashew Smoothie

This smoothie recipe with fig, banana, and cashew is healthy and delicious!

Preparation Time: 5 minutes
Total Time: 5 minutes
Yield: 2 servings

Ingredients

2 medium figs (pulp only, cut into small pieces)
1 medium banana (cut into small pieces)
2 Tbsp. cashew nuts
1 cup skim milk
1 cup ice cubes

Method

1. Combine the figs, banana, cashews, milk, and ice cubes in a blender. Process until it becomes smooth.
2. Pour and divide smoothie among 2 chilled glasses. Garnish with fig slices and serve with straw, if desired.
3. Enjoy.

Red Currant Cranberry and Yogurt Delight

This berry smoothie recipe has a nice tangy flavor that you will surely love.

Preparation Time: 5 minutes
Total Time: 5 minutes
Yield: 2 servings

Ingredients

1/2 cup of red currants
1/2 cup of cranberries
6 oz. low-fat yogurt
1 cup of ice cubes
2 tsp. agave nectar

Method

1. Combine the cranberries, red currants, low-fat yogurt, ice cubes, and agave nectar in a high-speed blender. Process until smooth.
2. Pour and divide among 2 chilled glasses.
3. Serve with straw and enjoy.

Minty Strawberry and Yogurt Smoothie

This traditional strawberry smoothie recipe is the perfect summertime drink!

Preparation Time: 5 minutes
Total Time: 5 minutes
Yield: 2 servings

Ingredients
1cup frozen strawberries (hulled and halved)

1/2 cup of skim milk
1/2 cup of Greek yogurt
1 Tbsp. peppermint syrup
fresh mint sprigs

Method
1.	Combine the strawberries, milk, yogurt, and peppermint syrup in a blender. Process until it becomes smooth.
2.	Pour and divide among 2 chilled glasses. Garnish with fresh mint sprigs.
3.	Serve and enjoy.

Pear Raspberry and Ricotta Smoothie

A decadent smoothie recipe made with pear, raspberry, and ricotta.

Preparation Time: 5 minutes
Total Time: 5 minutes
Yield: 2 servings

Ingredients
1 cup frozen raspberries
1 medium pear (peeled, cored, and cut into small pieces)
1 cup skim milk
1/2 cup ricotta cheese
fresh mint sprigs

Method
1. Combine the raspberries, pear, skim milk, and ricotta cheese in a blender. Process until it becomes smooth.
2. Pour and divide smoothie among 2 chilled glasses. Top with some raspberries and garnish with mint sprigs, if desired.
3. Serve immediately and enjoy.

Yummy Strawberry Ricotta Cooler

This smoothie recipe strawberries and ricotta is an absolute delight for the taste buds!

Preparation Time: 5 minutes
Total Time: 5 minutes
Yield: 2 servings

Ingredients
1 cup frozen strawberries (halved)
2/3 cup ricotta cheese
1 1/2 cup skim milk
2 Tbsp. strawberry syrup

Method
1. Combine the strawberries, ricotta cheese, skim milk, and strawberry syrup in a blender. Process until it becomes smooth.
2. Pour and divide mixture among 2 chilled glasses. Drizzle with more strawberry syrup on top to decorate, if desired.
3. Serve and enjoy.

Apple Banana and Peanut Butter Smoothie

This very delicious smoothie recipe is not only packed with flavor, but also rich in fiber, vitamins and minerals.

Preparation Time: 5 minutes
Total Time: 5 minutes
Yield: 2 servings

Ingredients

1 medium frozen banana (cut into small pieces)
1 medium apple (peeled, cored and cut into small pieces)
1 cup low-fat milk
2 Tbsp. peanut butter
1 Tbsp. honey
1 cup ice cubes
chopped peanuts

Method

1. Combine the banana, apple, milk, peanut butter, honey, and ice cubes in a high-speed blender. Process until smooth and creamy.
2. Pour and divide smoothie among 2 chilled glasses. Sprinkle with chopped peanuts.
3. Serve immediately and enjoy.

Banana Strawberry and Flax Smoothie

This great tasting smoothie recipe is made with banana, strawberries, milk, yogurt, flaxseeds, and agave nectar.

Preparation Time: 5 minutes
Total Time: 5 minutes
Yield: 2 servings

Ingredients
1 cup low-fat milk
1/2 cup low-fat vanilla yogurt
1 medium frozen banana (cut into small pieces)
1/2 cup frozen strawberries
1 Tbsp. flaxseeds
1 Tbsp. agave nectar

Method
1. Combine the milk, yogurt, banana, strawberries, flaxseeds, and agave nectar in a blender. Process until it becomes smooth.
2. Pour and divide smoothie among 2 chilled glasses.
3. Serve immediately and enjoy.

Easy Mango Cheesecake Smoothie

A thick and creamy smoothie that is perfect for the summer!

Preparation Time: 5 minutes
Total Time: 5 minutes
Yield: 2 servings

Ingredients

1 cup mango (diced)
1/2 cup ricotta cheese
1/2 cup skim milk
2 Tbsp. crushed grahams
1 Tbsp. honey
4-6 ice cubes

Method

1. Combine mango, ricotta cheese, skim milk, grahams, honey, and ice cubes in a blender. Process until it becomes smooth.
2. Pour and divide smoothie among 2 chilled glasses. Garnish with diced mangoes and mint sprigs, if desired.
3. Serve immediately and enjoy.

Banana Strawberry Cereal and Yogurt Smoothie

Banana, strawberry, yogurt, and cereal blends perfectly in this fantastic smoothie recipe.

Preparation Time: 5 minutes
Total Time: 5 minutes
Yield: 2 servings

Ingredients
1 medium frozen banana (cut into small pieces)
1/2 cup frozen strawberries (hulled and halved)
1 cup skim milk
6 oz. low-fat vanilla yogurt
2 Tbsp. granola
1 Tbsp. wheat germ

Method
1. Place banana, strawberries, milk, yogurt, granola, and wheat germ in a high-speed blender. Process until smooth and creamy.
2. Pour and divide among 2 chilled glasses.
3. Serve with straw and enjoy.

Blackberry Almond and Oat Cooler

This delicious smoothie with blackberries, almond milk, and rolled oats is good for the body because it is loaded with nutrients that can also boost your energy.

Preparation Time: 5 minutes
Total Time: 5 minutes
Yield: 2 servings

Ingredients
1 cup frozen blackberries
1 cup almond milk
1/2 cup low-fat yogurt
2 Tbsp. rolled oats
2 tsp. honey
fresh mint sprigs

Method
1. Combine the blackberries, almond milk, yogurt, oats, and honey in a blender. Process until it becomes smooth.
2. Pour and divide smoothie among 2 chilled glasses. Top with some blackberries and mint sprigs, if desired.
3. Serve immediately and enjoy.

Delightful Tofu Banana and Cinnamon Smoothie

This Vegan-friendly smoothie is bursting with flavor and nutrients.

Preparation Time: 5 minutes
Total Time: 5 minutes
Yield: 2 servings

Ingredients
2 medium frozen banana(cut into small pieces)
1/2 cup silken tofu
1/2 cup soy milk
1/2 soy yogurt (vanilla flavor)
1/4 tsp. cinnamon (ground)

Method
1. Place the banana, silken tofu, soy milk, soy yogurt, and cinnamon in a blender. Process in until it becomes smooth.
2. Pour and divide among 2 chilled glasses. Sprinkle with more cinnamon on top, if desired.
3. Serve and enjoy!

Strawberry Kiwi Milkshake

A delicious and refreshing tropical smoothie recipe made with pineapple, banana, and yogurt.

Preparation Time: 5 minutes
Total Time: 5 minutes
Yield: 2 servings

Ingredients
1 cup pineapple (cubed)
1 medium banana(cut into small pieces)
6 oz. low-fat yogurt (vanilla flavor)
4-6 ice cubes
fresh mint sprigs

Method
1. Combine the pineapple, banana, yogurt, and ice cubes in a high-speed blender. Process until it becomes smooth.
2. Pour smoothie in 2 chilled glasses. Garnish with a small slice of pineapple and mint sprigs, if desired.
3. Serve immediately and enjoy.

Berry Apple and Orange Smoothie

This scrumptious smoothie recipe with mixed berries, apple, orange, and yogurt will give you a good dose of antioxidants for stronger immune system.

Preparation Time: 5 minutes
Total Time: 5 minutes
Yield: 2 servings

Ingredients

1/2 cup blueberries
1/2 cup red currants
1 medium apple (cored and cut into small pieces)
1 medium seedless orange (peeled and cut into segments)
6 oz. Greek yogurt
4 ice cubes

Method

1. Place the blueberries, red currants, apple, orange, yogurt, and ice cubes in a high-speed blender. Process until smooth.
2. Pour smoothie in 2 chilled glasses. Top with few berries, is desired.
3. Serve immediately and enjoy.

Delicious and Healthy Green Smoothie

Drinking this amazing green smoothie regularly can help you lose weight and stay healthy.

Preparation Time: 5 minutes
Total Time: 5 minutes
Yield: 2 servings

Ingredients

1 medium apple (cored and cut into small pieces)
1 cup of chopped kale
1 cup of freshly squeezed orange juice
2 Tbsp. lemon juice
1 Tbsp. of flaxseeds
2 tsp. honey
1cup ice cubes

Method

1. Place the apple, kale, orange juice, lemon juice, flaxseeds, honey, and ice cubes in a high-speed blender. Process until smooth.
2. Pour smoothie in 2 chilled glasses.
3. Serve immediately and enjoy.

Black Currant Banana and Almond Smoothie

This healthy smoothie recipe with black currants, almond milk, and yogurt makes a great snack on the go.

Preparation Time: 5 minutes
Total Time: 5 minutes
Yield: 2 servings

Ingredients
1 cup black currants
2 medium frozen banana(cut into small pieces)
1 cup almond milk
1/4 tsp. pure vanilla extract
fresh mint sprigs

Method
1. Combine the black currants, banana, almond milk, and vanilla extract in a blender. Process until it becomes smooth.
2. Pour and divide smoothie among 2 chilled glasses. Garnish with few currants and mint sprigs.
3. Serve immediately and enjoy.

Easy Cardamom Raspberry and Pear Smoothie

This cardamom-spiced smoothie recipe with raspberries and pear is very is to make and so tasty.

Preparation Time: 5 minutes
Total Time: 5 minutes
Yield: 2 servings

Ingredients
1 cup fresh raspberries
1 medium pear (cored and cut into small pieces)
1 cup skim milk
1/4 tsp. cardamom
4 ice cubes
fresh mint sprigs

Method
1. Combine the raspberries, pear, milk, cardamom, and ice cubes in a blender. Process until it becomes smooth.
2. Pour smoothie in 2 chilled glasses. Garnish with mint sprigs.
3. Serve and enjoy.

Banana Cucumber Radish Smoothie with Parsley

If you are looking for a delicious green smoothie recipe, try this one!

Preparation Time: 5 minutes
Total Time: 5 minutes
Yield: 2 servings

Ingredients

2 medium frozen banana (cut into small pieces)
1/2 medium cucumber (cut into small pieces)
2 medium radishes (cut into small pieces)
6 oz. Greek yogurt (plain)
1/2 cup rice milk

Method

1. Place the banana, cucumber, radish, yogurt, and rice milk in a high-speed blender. Process until smooth.
2. Pour smoothie in 2 chilled glasses.
3. Serve immediately and enjoy.

Peach Banana and Cottage Cheese Smoothie

Both peach and banana are naturally sweet that when combined with cottage cheese and milk yields a decadent and satisfying drink.

Preparation Time: 5 minutes
Total Time: 5 minutes
Yield: 2 servings

Ingredients

2 peach halves(cut into small pieces)
1 medium frozen banana (cut into small pieces)
1 cupskim milk
1/2 cup cottage cheese
4 ice cubes

Method

1.   Place the peach halves, banana, milk, cottage cheese,and ice cubes in a high-speed blender. Process until smooth and creamy.
2.   Pour in 2 chilled glasses. Garnish with small slices of peach and mint sprig, if desired.
3.   Serve and enjoy.

Kiwi Banana Smoothie with Pumpkin Seed

This healthy smoothie with tropical flavor is can be enjoyed anytime of the day.

Preparation Time: 5 minutes
Total Time: 5 minutes
Yield: 2 servings

Ingredients
1 cup kiwi fruit(peeled and cubed)
1 medium banana (cut into small pieces)
1 cup skim milk
1 cup ice cubes
2 Tbsp. pumpkin seeds
fresh mint sprigs

Method
1.   Combine the kiwi, banana, skim milk, ice cubes, and pumpkin seeds in a high-speed blender. Process until it becomes smooth.
2.   Pour smoothie in 2 chilled glasses. Garnish with mint sprigs.
3.   Serve and enjoy.

Raspberry Cucumber and Rhubarb Smoothie

This scrumptious smoothie is a great way to get your daily dose of fiber and vitamins.

Preparation Time: 5 minutes
Total Time: 5 minutes
Yield: 2 servings

Ingredients
1 cup frozen raspberries
1/2 medium cucumber (peeled, deseeded and cut into small pieces)
2 rhubarb (cut into small pieces)
1 cup almond milk
1 Tbsp. honey

Method
1. Combine the raspberries, cucumber, rhubarb, almond milk, and honey in a blender. Process until it becomes smooth.
2. Pour and divide smoothie among 2 chilled glasses.
3. Serve and enjoy!

Purple Berry Smoothie

An excellent source of antioxidants, this healthy smoothie recipe combines the flavor and nutrition of blueberry, blackberry, and cranberry.

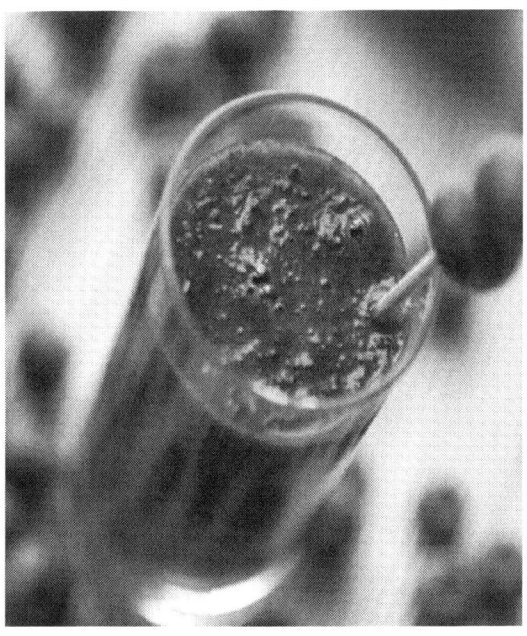

Preparation Time: 5 minutes
Total Time: 5 minutes
Yield: 3 servings

Ingredients
1 cup blueberries
1 cup blackberries
1 cup cranberry juice
1 cup ice cubes

Method
1. Place the berries, cranberry juice, and ice cubes in a high-speed blender. Process until smooth.
2. Pour smoothie in 3 chilled glasses.
3. Serve and enjoy.

Quick and Easy Fruit Cooler

A refreshing smoothie that can also give you an energy boost when you need one.

Preparation Time: 5 minutes
Total Time: 5 minutes
Yield: 3 servings

Ingredients
1 medium apple (cored and diced)
1 medium banana (cut into small pieces)
1/2 cup strawberries
1/2 cup blackberries
1 cup skim milk
1 cup ice cubes

Method
1. Combine the apple, banana, strawberries, blackberries, milk, and ice cubes in a blender. Process until it becomes smooth.
2. Pour smoothie in chilled glasses.
3. Serve and enjoy.

Fruit Cereal and Almond Smoothie

It is a delectable and nutrient packed smoothie recipe that is perfect for breakfast.

Preparation Time: 5 minutes
Total Time: 5 minutes
Yield: 2 servings

Ingredients
1 cup almond milk
1 medium frozen banana, cut into small pieces
1/2 cup frozen strawberries
1/2 cup mango (diced)
2 Tbsp. oat bran
2 Tbsp. wheat germ

Method
1.   Combine the almond milk, banana, strawberries, mango, oat bran, and wheat germ in a blender. Process until smooth and creamy.
2.   Pour smoothie in 2 chilled glasses. Garnish with strawberries, if desired.
3.   Serve and enjoy.

Luscious Banana-Mango Yogurt Smoothie

This smoothie recipe with banana, mango, and yogurt is so yummy!

Preparation Time: 5 minutes
Total Time: 5 minutes
Yield: 3 servings

Ingredients

1 medium banana (cut into small pieces)
1 cup mango (diced)
1 cup Greek yogurt
1 cup low-fat milk
1 cup ice cubes

Method

1. Place the banana, mango, yogurt, milk, and ice cubes in a high-speed blender. Process until smooth and creamy.
2. Pour and divide smoothie among 3chilled glasses. Garnish with a small slice of mango and serve with straw, if desired.
3. Enjoy.

Almond Mango and Dragon Fruit Smoothie

Fast and easy smoothie recipe that is also good for your health!

Preparation Time: 5 minutes
Total Time: 5 minutes
Yield: 3 servings

Ingredients
2medium dragon fruit
1 cup of mango (cubed)

1 1/2 cup almond milk
1 cup ice cubes
fresh mint sprigs

Method

1.   Combine the dragon fruit, mango, almond milk, and ice cubes in a blender. Process until it becomes smooth.

2.   Pour smoothie in 3 chilled glasses. Garnish with fresh mint sprigs.

3.   Serve immediately and enjoy.

Pineapple Mango and Coconut Smoothie

You will surely love this super delicious smoothie made with pineapple, mango, and coconut water.

Preparation Time: 5 minutes
Total Time: 5 minutes
Yield: 3 servings

Ingredients

1 cup pineapple (cubed)
1 cup mango (diced)
1 cup coconut water
1 cup ice cubes

Method

1. Combine the pineapple, mango, coconut water, and ice cubes in a blender. Process until it becomes smooth.
2. Pour the smoothie in 3 chilled glasses and serve with decorative straw, if desired.
3. Serve and enjoy.

Les Ilagan

Pineapple Peach and Coconut Smoothie

An awesome smoothie recipe that will bring you to a tropical island.

Preparation Time: 5 minutes
Total Time: 5 minutes
Yield: 3 servings

Ingredients
1 cup frozen pineapple (cubed)
1 medium frozen banana (cut into small pieces)
2 peach halves (cubed)
1 cup coconut water
1 cup ice cubes
1/3 cup coconut milk
1 Tbsp. honey

Method
1. Place the pineapple, banana, peach halves, coconut water, coconut milk, and honey in a blender. Process until smooth.
2. Pour smoothie in 3chilled glasses and garnish with small slices of pineapple and peach, if desired.
3. Serve immediately and enjoy.

Beet Dragon Fruit and Coconut Smoothie with Chia

This flavorful smoothie with beet, dragon fruit, coconut, and chia is a great way to beat the summer heat!

Preparation Time: 5 minutes
Total Time: 5 minutes
Yield: 2 servings

Ingredients
2 medium beets (cut into small pieces)
11/2 medium dragon fruit (peeled and cut into small pieces)
1 cup coconut water
1 cup crushed ice
1 Tbsp. chia seeds
fresh mint sprigs

Method
1.	Combine the dragon fruit, beets, coconut water, ice, and chia in a blender. Process until it becomes smooth.
2.	Pour smoothie in 2 chilled glasses. Garnish with fresh mint sprigs.
3.	Serve and enjoy.

Vegan Strawberry Smoothie with Walnuts

This smoothie combines the flavor of strawberries, rice milk, maple syrup, and walnuts. A must try recipe!

Preparation Time: 5 minutes
Total Time: 5 minutes
Yield: 2 servings

Ingredients
1cup frozen strawberries
11/2 cup rice milk
1 Tbsp. maple syrup
1/4 cup chopped walnuts
fresh mint sprigs

Method
1.	Place the strawberries, rice milk, maple syrup, and walnuts in a high-speed blender. Process until smooth.
2.	Pour smoothie in 2 chilled glasses.
3.	Serve immediately and enjoy.

Cranberry Soy Breakfast Smoothie

This smoothie recipe with cranberries, soy yogurt, soy milk, and cereals is very rich in fiber, vitamins and minerals.

Preparation Time: 5 minutes
Total Time: 5 minutes
Yield: 2 servings

Ingredients
1 cup frozen cranberries
6 oz. soy yogurt
1/2 cup soy milk
2 Tbsp. oat bran
1 Tbsp. wheat germ
1 Tbsp. honey

Method
1. Place the cranberries, soy yogurt, soy milk, oat bran, wheat germ, and honey in a blender. Process until it becomes smooth.
2. Pour smoothie in 2 chilled glasses. Garnish with few cranberries, if desired.
3. Serve immediately and enjoy.

Dark Choco Banana and Peanut Butter Smoothie

Super delicious smoothie recipe made with dark chocolate, banana, and peanut butter!

Preparation Time: 5 minutes
Total Time: 5 minutes
Yield: 2 servings

Ingredients
1 1/2 cup skim milk
2 oz. dark chocolate sauce
1 medium banana (cut into small pieces)
2 Tbsp. peanut butter
1/2 cup crushed ice
chocolate shavings

Method
1.	Place the milk, dark chocolate sauce, peanut butter, and crushed ice in a high-speed blender. Process until smooth.
2.	Pour smoothie in 2 chilled glasses. Top with some chocolate shavings.
3.	Serve immediately and enjoy.

Watermelon Coconut Smoothie with Hemp Seed

If you are in search for a great tasting summer refreshment, this is the recipe for you!

Preparation Time: 5 minutes
Total Time: 5 minutes
Yield: 2 servings

Ingredients
1 cup watermelon (cubed)
1 cup coconut water

2 Tbsp. lemon juice
2 tsp. hemp seeds
2 tsp. agave nectar
4 ice cubes

Method

1. Combine the watermelon, coconut water, lemon juice, hemp seeds, agave nectar, and ice cubes in a blender. Process until mixture becomes smooth.
2. Pour smoothie in 2 chilled glasses.
3. Serve immediately and enjoy.

Papaya Citrus Cooler with Honey

A delicious blend of flavor from papaya, orange, lime, and honey.

Preparation Time: 5 minutes
Total Time: 5 minutes
Yield: 2 servings

Ingredients

1 cup papaya (cubed)
1 cup freshly squeezed orange juice

2 Tbsp. lime juice
1 Tbsp. honey
1 cup ice cubes

Method

1. Combine the papaya, orange juice, lime juice, honey, and ice cubes in a blender. Process until mixture becomes smooth.

2. Pour smoothie in 2 chilled glasses. Garnish with a slice of lime, if desired.

3. Serve and enjoy.

Peach Strawberry and Almond Smoothie with Flax

Peach, strawberries, and almond milk when combined together yields a great tasting and healthy drink.

Preparation Time: 5 minutes
Total Time: 5 minutes
Yield: 2 servings

Ingredients
2 peach halves (diced)
1 cup fresh strawberries (halved)
1 cup almond milk
1 Tbsp. flaxseeds
4-6 ice cubes

Method
1. Place the peach halves, strawberries, almond milk, flaxseeds, and ice cubes in a high-speed blender. Process until smooth and creamy.
2. Pour smoothie in 2 chilled glasses. Garnish with peach and strawberry slices, if desired.
3. Serve immediately and enjoy.

Breakfast Choco Banana Protein Smoothie

A perfect smoothie to drink before going to the gym.

Preparation Time: 5 minutes
Total Time: 5 minutes
Yield: 2 servings

Ingredients
2 scoops chocolate protein powder
1 medium frozen banana

2 cups almond milk
2 Tbsp. oat bran
1/4 tsp. cinnamon (ground)

Method

1.	Combine the chocolate powder, banana, almond milk, oat bran, and cinnamon in a blender and process until well blended and smooth.
2.	Pour smoothie in 2 chilled glasses.
3.	Serve immediately and enjoy.

Easy Avocado Soy and Maple Smoothie

A rejuvenating smoothie recipe that is loaded with wonderful flavors from avocado, soy milk, and maple syrup.

Preparation Time: 5 minutes
Total Time: 5 minutes
Yield: 2 servings

Ingredients
1/2 cup avocado (diced)
1 cup soy milk

1cup crushed ice
1 Tbsp. maple syrup
fresh mint sprig

Method

1. Place the avocado, soy milk, crushed ice, and maple syrup in a high-speed blender. Process until smooth and creamy.
2. Pour smoothie in 2 chilled glasses. Garnish with mint sprig, if desired.
3. Serve immediately and enjoy.

Strawberry Plum and Coconut Smoothie with Chia

An awesome treat for everyone, this recipe is very tasty and healthy!

Preparation Time: 5 minutes
Total Time: 5 minutes
Yield: 2 servings

Ingredients

1 cup strawberries
2 medium plum (pitted)
1 1/2 cup coconut water
2 tsp. chia seeds
4-6 ice cubes

Method

1. Place the strawberries, plum, coconut water, chia seeds, and ice cubes in a blender. Process until it becomes smooth.
2. Pour smoothie in 2 chilled glasses.
3. Serve immediately and enjoy.

Printed in Great Britain
by Amazon